Wide Range
Starters
Green Book 2

Phyllis Flowerdew

Oliver & Boyd

Illustrated by Shirley Bellwood, Jon Davis,
John Harrold, Donald Harley and Dave Simmonds

Oliver & Boyd
Longman House
Burnt Mill
Harlow
Essex CM20 2JE

An Imprint of Longman Group UK Ltd

First published 1985
Fifth impression 1990

© Phyllis Flowerdew 1985
All rights reserved; no part of this publication
may be reproduced, stored in a retrieval system,
or transmitted in any form or by any means,
electronic, mechanical, photocopying,
recording, or otherwise without either the prior
written permission of the Publishers or a licence
permitting restricted copying in the United Kingdom
issued by the Copyright Licensing Agency Ltd,
33-34 Alfred Place, London, WC1E 7DP.

ISBN 0 05 003721 8

Set in 16/24 point Monophoto Plantin
Produced by Longman Group (FE) Ltd
Printed in Hong Kong

Where to find the Stories

Page

4 The Car Wash

15 The Pedlar's Dream

28 The Ice Cream Van

33 The Boy and the Bear

43 The Black Dog

55 Strong Boy

The Car Wash

Mini the Motor Car belonged to Mr Patel. Every week he took her to the petrol station to get petrol.

Every week while she was there, Mini saw a car go into the car wash.

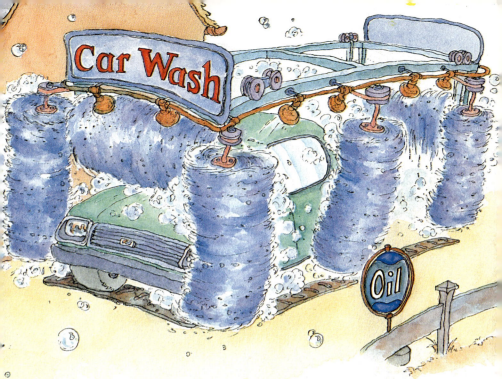

She saw the big, blue brushes
rolling backwards and forwards
and up and down.
She saw them swishing and swoshing
and splashing and spraying.
"I hope I never have to go
into the car wash,"
she said to herself.
"I hope I never, never, have to go
into the car wash."

Now Mr Patel
kept Mini the Motor Car
very clean and shiny.

"I can keep her
clean and shiny myself,"
he said. "So why pay money
to put her in the car wash?"

But one wet day
Mr Patel and Mini the Motor Car
had to call at a farm.
It was quite a long way
out of the town,
and the roads were muddy.

The nearer Mr Patel and Mini
came to the farm,
the more and more muddy
the roads became.
And the last road of all
was just a narrow lane
that was wet with puddles
and THICK with mud.

Water and mud
splashed up Mini's sides.
Mud stuck to her wheels.
Mud stuck to her bumpers.
It even hid her lamps
and her number plates.
She looked very, very dirty.

On the way home,
Mr Patel said,

"We'll have to call
at the petrol station
and take you into the car wash
before the mud dries hard."

"Oh no," said Mini to herself.
"I won't go into the car wash.
I won't, I won't, I won't."
Soon they came to the petrol station.
"Hallo Mr Patel," said the petrol man.
"Mini's in a mess today."
"Yes," said Mr Patel,
"we've been on some very muddy roads.
I'll have to take Mini
into the car wash,"
and he drove her up to it.
"Oh no," said Mini to herself.
"I won't go into the car wash.
I won't. I won't. I won't,"
and she stopped.
She stood quite still
just before she came
to the big, blue brushes.

The big, blue brushes
were all ready
to roll backwards and forwards
and up and down.
They were all ready
to go swishing and swoshing
and splashing and spraying
over Mini the Motor Car.

But Mini the Motor Car wouldn't go in.
Mr Patel tried and tried
to get her to go forwards,
but she wouldn't move.

So Mr Patel tried going backwards.
Oh yes! That was fine!
Mini went backwards all right.

"Now try going forwards again,"
said the petrol man.

So Mr Patel tried
going forwards again.
Oh yes! Mini went forwards all right,
but she stopped
just before she came
to the big, blue brushes.
Mr Patel tried and tried
to get her to go
into the car wash,
but she wouldn't move.

"There must be something
wrong with her," he said.
"We'd better push her in
and get her clean,
and then I'll have to leave her here."

"Right," said the petrol man,
and he and Mr Patel pushed and pushed.
They pushed Mini the Motor Car
into the car wash.

The big, blue brushes
rolled backwards and forwards
and up and down over Mini.
The big, blue brushes
went swishing and swoshing
and splashing and spraying
over Mini the Motor Car.

She was still saying,
"I won't go in. I won't. I won't."
but as soon as she was really in,
she began to laugh.

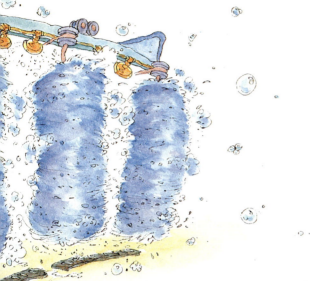

"I like it," she said. "I like it.
I like the car wash after all."

When Mr Patel and the petrol man
pushed her out again,
she was dripping wet,
but all the mud had been washed away
and she was clean and shiny once more.

Then Mr Patel
drove her three times
round the petrol station,
without any trouble at all.

"She seems to be all right now,"
he said.

"I think I know
what was wrong with her,"
said the petrol man.
"Anyway, I hope you get home safely."

And of course they did,
for the sun was shining
and Mini the Motor Car
was as happy as could be.

The Pedlar's Dream

There was once a poor pedlar
who lived in Norfolk.
He and his wife
had a cottage
with a small garden at the back.
In the garden
was a very big oak tree.

One night the pedlar had a dream.
In his dream, a voice said,
"Go to London Town.
Stand on London Bridge
and you will find a treasure."

In the morning
he told his wife
about the dream.
"Perhaps it will come true,"
she said.
"Oh no," said the pedlar.
"It is silly
to believe in dreams.
After all, dreams are only dreams.
But I think I will go to London
all the same."

The next day he set off.
It was a long way to go.
He walked most of the way,
but sometimes
he had a lift on a cart.
At night he slept in fields
or on haystacks.

Then after about four days
he came to London.
   "Here I am in London Town,"
he said,
"and there is London Bridge."
   He went on to London Bridge
and stood in the middle of it.

He looked all round,
but there was no treasure
to be seen.

Just then a man came along.

"Have you lost something?" he said.

"No," said the pedlar,
"but I had a dream the other night.
In my dream, a voice said,
'Go to London Town.
Stand on London Bridge
and you will find a treasure.'
So here I am,
but I can see no treasure."

"It is silly to believe in dreams,"
said the man. "After all,
dreams are only dreams.
I had a dream the other night.
It was about a pedlar's cottage
in Norfolk.

I was standing under a big oak tree
in the garden.
I was digging, digging, digging,
and I found a box
full of gold coins.
I don't know why
I should dream that.
I have never even been to Norfolk.
It is silly to believe in dreams.
After all, dreams are only dreams."

"Yes," said the pedlar,
and he began to walk back home.

After about four days
he came to his cottage.
He went into the garden
and began to dig
under the big oak tree.
He dug and dug and dug.

After a while,
his spade hit something hard,
and there he found a box
full of gold coins.
He could hardly believe his eyes!

After that, the pedlar and his wife
were never poor any more.
They moved to a bigger cottage,
and they gave a lot of money
to the church,
because it needed

a new steeple
and a new floor
and some new windows
and new seats.

They also gave the church
two gold candlesticks
and two small silver ships
to hold the incense.

Much of this story
must be true,
because in that church today
there is an old book
telling about these gifts,
and there is a carving
of the pedlar and his wife
and his children.

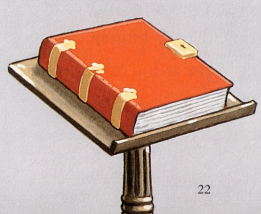

The Ice Cream Van

The ice cream van
came along the street,
ringing its bell,
  "Ding, dong, ding.
Ding, dong, ding."
  Kammie was on her way
to the shops
to buy some bread.
She was holding the hand
of her little sister Kim.
Kim was three years old.

"I'd like an ice cream," she said.

"Not today," said Kammie. "No money today."

The ice cream van stopped close by, and lots of children came running up. Mr Antonio, the ice cream man, jumped down from the driving seat, and opened the door at the back and the window at the side.

"Hallo, hallo," he said. "Nice ice cream today. Ice cream cornets, ice cream wafers, ice cream tubs. Yellow ice cream, pink ice cream, green ice cream, chocolate ice cream."

"Yummy, yummy," said the children.

Mr Antonio waited for them to come up with their money, but nobody came.

"Who's going to be first?" he said, but still nobody came.

Nobody had any money today.

Poor Mr Antonio could see that this was going to be a bad day.

Kammie and Kim
went on their way to the shops.
They went into the baker's,
but they had to wait a long time
to be served.

Suddenly Kammie found
that Kim had gone!

"She must be waiting outside,"
she thought, and she went on
waiting for her bread.

But Kim ran back
to the ice cream van.
It was still there,
but at that moment
Mr Antonio looked round and said,

"Well, nobody seems
to have any money today.
It's no good waiting.
I'll go on to the next town."
But before he went,

he had to take a box
of ice cream tubs
to a shop across the road.
He closed the window
and took the box
out of the door at the back.
 Bad little Kim saw
that the door was open,
so she climbed inside the van
to have a look round.

In a moment,
Mr Antonio came back.
He banged the door
and locked it.
Then he went into the driving seat
and drove away.
The children stood
and watched him go.
 Then along came Kammie
with her loaf of bread.

 "Where's Kim?" she said.
 "She was here just now,"
said a boy.
 "She must have gone home,"
said a girl.

So Kammie ran home,
but Kim was not there.
Kammie went
to the house next door,
but Kim was not there.
Where could she be?
  Soon lots of people
were looking for her.
The children were looking.
The mothers were looking.
Where was Kim?
Where was Kim?

Suddenly there was
a ding, dong, ding,
ding, dong, ding.
"The ice cream van
has come back!"
said the children.
It stopped close by,
and Mr Antonio jumped down
from the driving seat.
 Then he lifted someone else down.
It was Kim!
 "Look who I found
when I opened the van
at the next town,"
said Mr Antonio.
"She was crying and screaming,
but of course
I hadn't heard her
while I was driving."
 "Kim!" said Kammie.

"Poor Mr Antonio,
wasting his time,"
said one of the mothers,
and she asked for two ice creams
for her children.

So Mr Antonio
opened the window
at the side of the van.

Then other mothers
bought ice creams for their children too.

"Just because we're glad
that Kim is safe," they said.

So Mr Antonio didn't have
such a bad day after all.

And Kim?
Well, someone bought her
an ice cream too,
though she didn't really
deserve it, did she?

The Boy and the Bear

This is an old, old story
that is told in many lands.

One day, at the end of the summer,
an Eskimo woman
was picking berries.
She had her baby on her back,
and he was fast asleep.

There were not many berries
left on the bushes,
and she had to walk a long way
looking for them.

The baby grew heavy
so she put him down
just inside a cave,
and left him there.

Soon, when she had picked
all the berries she could find,
she went back
to get the baby.

She looked inside the cave,
but the baby was not there.
She called out to him
but there was no answer.

She started to go inside the cave,
but she was stopped
by an angry roar!
The cave belonged to a bear,
and she knew it would kill her
if she went in any further.

"Oh dear! Oh dear!" she cried.
"The bear must have killed my baby,"

and she went home,
weeping and wailing.

Now the bear
had once had cubs,
so when she found the baby,
she looked after him
as if he had been
a little bear cub.

She carried him gently
to the back of the cave,
and she gave him
small bits of meat to eat.
Every day she left him there
while she went out hunting,
and the baby kept warm
by lying among the fur skins
of the animals
the bear had killed.

All through the winter
the bear kept the baby safe
in the cave.

All through the winter
everything was white with snow.
Sometimes the baby tried
to crawl out to look at it,
but the big bear
always pushed him back
with her big, soft paw.

When spring came, the snow melted,
and by that time
the baby had learned to walk.
Then the bear took him out
in the sunshine
and showed him some of the animals
that lived among the rocks
and bushes.
He saw little mice and squirrels,
and deer and foxes and wolves.

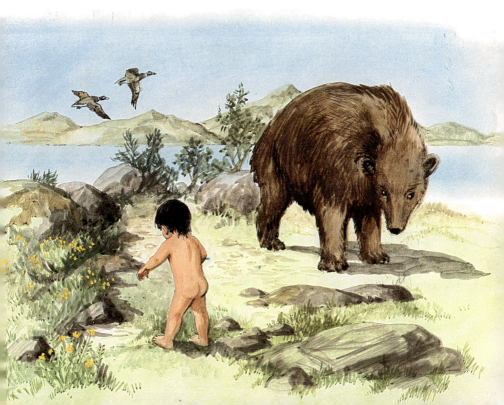

As he grew older and bigger,
the bear mother showed him
how to hunt the smaller animals.
 She took him
to some of her secret places,
but she never took him near the sea.
She never took him
near the cold, grey waters
where the whales swam
and the seals dived and played.

Then one day,
when the boy was seven years old,
he went for a walk by himself.
The bear was asleep
and she didn't see him go.
He wrapped himself in a fur,
and he walked a long way
until he came to the sea.

There were some people
standing on the shore.
The boy did not think
he had ever seen people before.
He thought they must be animals.
But what sort of animals were they?

They were not deer or foxes.
They were not wolves or bears.
What could they be?

He hid behind a rock
and watched them.

"They look a bit like me,"
he thought,
and then he ran back to the cave
and his bear mother.

A few days later,
he walked to the sea a second time.
There on the shore
he saw people again.
They had been catching fish
and they had two small boats
at the edge of the water.

The boy wanted
to have a good look at them,
so he went a bit nearer,
and a bit nearer.

Suddenly someone said,
"Who is this?"
Then the people crowded round him
in a friendly and puzzled way.

"He is like my daughter,"
said one old man.
"He could be —
he must be the child
who was taken by a bear."
The people took him back
to their village
and they brought his own parents
to see him.
They spoke to him
by using signs,
and soon he understood
that he really belonged to them.
So he lived with his real mother
and father again,
and he grew up happily
with his own people.

Adapted

The Black Dog

There was a knock at the door.
Dad went to answer it,
with Emma close behind.

A man stood outside.

"Have you seen a black dog?"
he asked.

"No," said Dad.

"Oh dear," said the man.

"I've been looking for him for
about two hours now.
I was driving home
when a car crashed into mine.
Luckily no one was hurt,
but both cars were dented a bit.
My dog was in the back seat.

The door flew open
and he was thrown out.
He was frightened,
and he ran and ran
across the fields.
I don't like leaving him,
but it's getting dark now,
and I must go home."

"We'll keep a look out for him,"
said Dad.
The man took a bit of paper
out of his pocket.

"I'll give you my phone number,"
he said, and he wrote,

"John Carter, 5438,"
and gave it to Dad.

"The dog's name is Ricky," he said.

Then he climbed into his dented car
and drove slowly away.

"Poor dog," said Emma.
"He might be hurt.
He might be lying in a field
not able to walk
any more."

Before she went to bed
that night,
Emma went to the back door
and looked out
across the dark fields,
and called loudly,
"Ricky, Ricky, Ricky!"

She hoped and hoped
that a black dog
would come running up,
but all she heard
was an owl
hooting and hooting
in a tree.

Next morning
she and Dad got up early
and went for a walk
before school.
They did not have time
to go very far,
but they looked and looked,
and they called loudly,
"Ricky, Ricky, Ricky!"

They hoped and hoped that
a black dog would come running up.
But all they heard
was the morning traffic driving
along the road.

After school that day,
Emma and Mum
had a walk with
Emma's baby brother.
They called and called
and looked and looked,
but the black dog
was not to be seen.

Before she went to bed
that night,
Emma went to the back door
and looked out again
across the dark fields.
She called loudly,
"Ricky, Ricky, Ricky!"
She hoped and hoped
that a black dog
would come running up,
but all she saw
was a prickly hedgehog
taking a walk in the grass.

Then, in the night,
Emma woke up suddenly.
She could hear something.
It sounded like crying.
Perhaps it was her baby brother.
But no.
It sounded more like an animal.
It sounded like a dog.

She crept to the window
and looked out.

She could see nothing
but darkness
and shadows.

Then she heard the first birds
starting to sing.
Morning would soon be here.
Then she could wake Dad.
She went back to bed
and waited
and listened.

It seemed a long time
till the sky began
to grow light,
and the birds sang
their loud morning song.

Emma crept to Mum and Dad's room.
She went very quietly
so that she didn't wake
the baby.

"Dad," she whispered,
"I think the dog must be near.
I can hear him crying."
　A little later,
Emma and Dad
were walking in the fields
nearer and nearer to the place
where the sound of crying
came from.
　And there, lying in a dry ditch,
they found Ricky.
He was crying and shivering,
and he had a big gash
in his side.

"Ricky, Ricky," said Emma,
and he lifted his black head
and licked her hand.

Dad phoned Mr Carter,
and he came that morning
with a vet,
and took Ricky home.

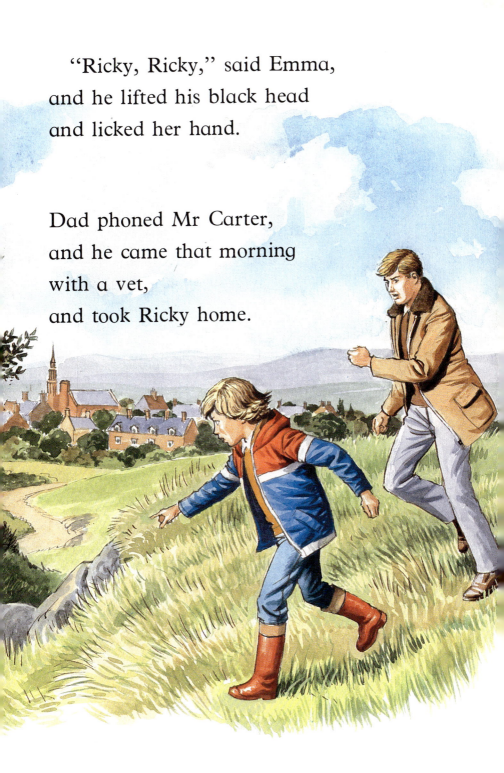

A few months later
Mr Carter called at the cottage.
Ricky was with him,
black and frisky and well again.
He held a parcel in his mouth.

"Take it, Emma," said Mr Carter.
"It's for you and your kind family."

So Emma took it,
and unwrapped it,
and found a lovely box of chocolates
"with love from Ricky."

Strong Boy

Once upon a time
there was a Red Indian boy.
His friends called him Strong Boy,
but his mother and father
often called him Lazy Boy.
    He was quiet and dreamy
and he did not often play
with other children.
Perhaps it was because
he sometimes hurt other boys
without meaning to hurt them.
    Perhaps it was because
he could so easily win
most of the games.
It wasn't really much fun for him
to be so strong.

In the summer
he liked to walk alone
in the fields and forests.
In the winter
he liked to sit in the wigwam
over the warm ashes of the fire.

One day when it was very cold,
his mother had been fishing
through a hole in the ice.
She brought the fish home
and hung the fishing nets
outside the door.
They were dripping and freezing.

She saw Strong Boy
sitting by the fire.

"You're so lazy," she said.
"You never help me
with my work.
Go and wring the nets for me
and take them into
the sunshine to dry."

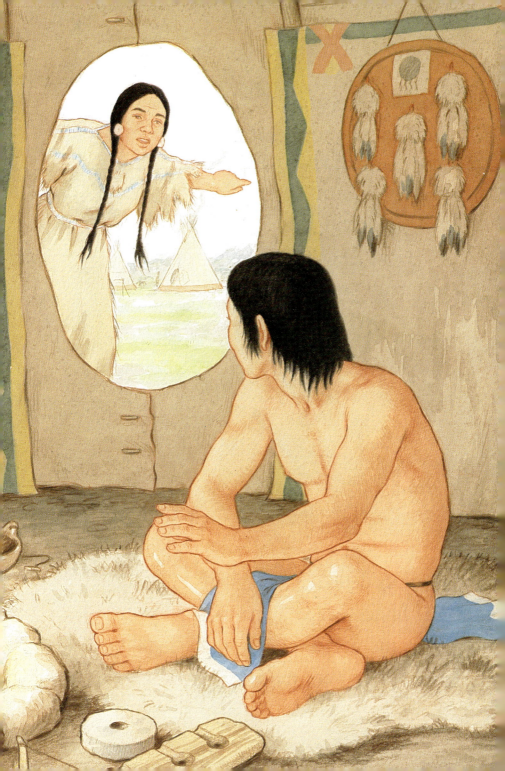

Slowly, Strong Boy stood up
and left the fire
and left the wigwam.
He took hold of the nets
that hung outside the door,
dripping and freezing.

He wrung them gently,
as gently as he could.

But oh dear,
his fingers were so strong
that the nets broke
as if they were made of straw.

One day his father was going hunting. He saw Strong Boy sitting by the fire in the wigwam.

"You're so lazy," he said. "You never help me with the hunting; and when you do, you break every bow and arrow that you touch.

But come with me,
and you can carry home
the deer or bison
that we will kill for food."

So Strong Boy went with his father.
They walked beside a stream
in a narrow valley.
They could see the trail
of deer and bison
in the soft mud
at the side of the water.

After a while
they came to a great pile of trees
that had been blown across their path.
Pine trees and cedar trees
were lying on top of each other.
"We'll have to go back,"
said Strong Boy's father.
"We can't climb over all these trees.
Even a squirrel couldn't get over
all these tree trunks
and logs and branches."

The father sat down to rest.
He lit his pipe
and puffed smoke into the air.
But Strong Boy
lifted the tree trunks
and threw them out of the way
as if they were as light as arrows.

He threw pine trees and cedar trees
to the right and to the left.
He cleared the way
before his father had even
finished his pipe.

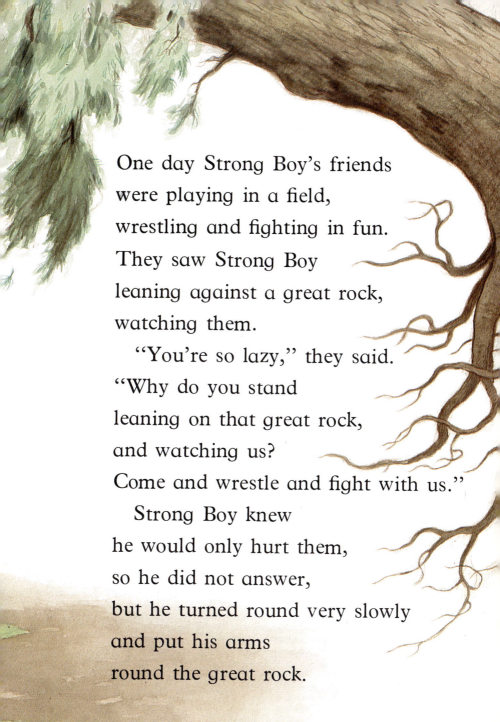

One day Strong Boy's friends
were playing in a field,
wrestling and fighting in fun.
They saw Strong Boy
leaning against a great rock,
watching them.

"You're so lazy," they said.
"Why do you stand
leaning on that great rock,
and watching us?
Come and wrestle and fight with us."

Strong Boy knew
he would only hurt them,
so he did not answer,
but he turned round very slowly
and put his arms
round the great rock.

He tore it from the earth
as if it were just a pebble.
He held it a moment
high above his head.
Then he threw it
far, far into the river,
and there it stayed always
for everyone to see.

Adapted from "Hiawatha"